How to Organize an Effective Team Teaching Program

How to Organize an Effective Team Teaching Program

by Harold S. Davis

Dr. Davis is director of in-service education and staff utilization for the Educational Research Council of Greater Cleveland. He serves as consultant to superintendents and principals in more than 30 school districts located in Massachusetts, Michigan, Minnesota, New York, and Ohio. He has advised on building design, scheduling, and team organization for many of the projects described in this booklet.

He has many years of service as a teacher, counselor and school administrator. In recent years, he served as educational consultant to the Department of the Navy's College ROTC program and as director of the Artillery School in Detroit, Michigan.

He is a frequent lecturer on university campuses, a co-author of the book *Instructional Materials Center; Bold New Venture*, 1966, and author of numerous pamphlets and articles on staff utilization and team teaching.

SUCCESSFUL SCHOOL MANAGEMENT SERIES

Prentice-Hall, Inc.

Library of Congress Catalog Card Number:
66-19895

Printed in the United States of America
42549—X

Foreword

The *idea* of team teaching is not new. What is new is the *extension* of team teaching—more schools at all levels of education are exploring this approach toward improving educational opportunities.

There are several reasons why this is so. Team teaching potentially provides more attention to the systematic organization of instruction; it contains the promise of more teacher and student interest in learning; it emphasizes more imaginative methodology; and it can effectively reduce the boredom that occurs when students are required to memorize what a teacher says.

All would be well, of course, if there were enough really effective teachers to go around. But there are not, and herein lies both our difficulty and our challenge. This book properly points out that team teaching, regardless of how it is defined or used, is one of the major imaginative and realistic approaches to better teaching and learning.

Ellsworth Tompkins
Executive Secretary
National Association of
Secondary-School
Principals

Contents

7

TEAM teaching is a phenomenon

in American Education. It has undergone a steady, rapid growth. In fact, an NEA poll of 1400 elementary and secondary school principals showed the following growth in the use of teaching teams:

	Elementary	Secondary
1955	5%	5%
1960	15	12
1965	30	31

What Is Team Teaching?

Although there are almost as many variations as there are teams, all team teaching is based on the premise that teachers can accomplish more working together than working alone. *Team teaching is any form of teaching in which two or more teachers regularly and purposefully share responsibility for the planning, presentation, and evaluation of lessons prepared for two or more classes of students.*

The key words in this definition are "regularly and purposefully share." Too many schools are prone to assemble children in the auditorium for a movie or lecture and then announce that they are engaged in team teaching. Some are under the mistaken impression that an exchange of classes constitutes team teaching. Others, at the elementary level confuse departmentalization with team teaching. Although such plans recognize the special abilities of teachers, none fit the definition.

11

In such programs, teachers continue to work as independent agents. In contrast, team teaching assumes that the "whole" of the participants *working together* will make a greater contribution than the "sum" of the individuals working alone.

Team teaching is an organizational pattern, within which the school can greatly improve the quality of its instructional program. As will be evident from this booklet, the team composed of two or more teachers goes hand-in-hand with instructional improvement through (1) better utilization of staff, (2) greater flexibility in grouping, scheduling, and the use of space, (3) provision for large-group, small-group, and individual instruction, and (4) increased use of audiovisual aids.

As every observer of change in the nation's public schools knows, the basic concepts of team teaching are not entirely new. A few secondary schools involved in the Progressive Education Association's "Eight Year Study" experimented with organizational patterns similar to team teaching, and some elementary schools had used the principles of flexible grouping. Moreover, a number of universities had tapped the talents of outstanding professors for large-group instruction and had followed with small seminars for discussion. And, in preparation for World War II, the armed forces made tremendous use of audiovisual aids, including educational films and filmstrips, overhead projectors, and language laboratories.

These innovations did have some influence on the nation's elementary and secondary schools, but education was somewhat of a laggard when it came to introducing them on a widespread scale. Though an effective organizational pattern was badly needed to implement change, its evolution took a considerable period of time.

• In 1956, NASSP, aided by the Ford Foundation and the Fund for the Advancement of Education, appointed its Staff Utilization Commission to discover, by study and experimentation, new and more effective means of staff utilization. Among the experiments, the one showing the most promise and given greatest attention was popularly called *team teaching*. By 1959, the Commission's capable administrator, J. Lloyd Trump, was able to state that the Commission had "stimulated sufficient momentum of interest among teachers and administrators" and that "continued support of experimentation by the Commission itself is no longer necessary." [1]

J. Lloyd Trump's prediction has been borne out by the facts. Team teaching is rapidly being introduced into the nation's schools. It is no longer experimental. It has been in use for years, and educators know that it works.

Types of Teams

Despite many variations, only two major types of teaching teams have evolved. We shall refer to them as *hierarchic* and *synergetic* teams.

● *Hierarchic teams*. We can liken the hierarchic team to a pyramid with the team leader at the apex, master teachers just below, and regular teachers at the base assisted by interns and aides. A major purpose of the hierarchy is to provide teachers with a means of professional advancement without having to leave the classroom. Well-known examples of this type of team are found in Lexington, Massachusetts; Pittsburgh, Pennsylvania; and in the Claremont program in southern California.

Although hierarchic teams offer many advantages, they embody some disadvantages. Many educators are inclined to feel that establishing levels tends to diminish the importance of the regular teacher's role, though supporters of the hierarchic arrangement claim that the teacher does not relinquish status in such a team.

Moreover, hierarchic teaching teams are not suited to the majority of our schools, for most superintendents and principals cannot replace present facilities or staff. They cannot expect foundation grants or help from universities, such as the schools mentioned above received, and they cannot afford to hire paraprofessional help. When looking for ways to improve instruction, they recognize that they must seek them within practical limits. Synergetic teams supply the answer.

● *Synergetic teams*. Synergetic teams are formed by two or more teachers willing to cooperate as professional equals. Such teams may be developed to work within conventional facili-

---

[1] "Completing the Commission's Staff Utilization Studies," *Bulletin* of the NASSP, January 1960, p. 345.

ties and schedules. All it takes is *leadership, perseverance,* and *perspiration.*

On a synergetic team, the master teacher concept is repudiated and instructional leadership rotates according to need. For example, one member may assume the leadership for a single lesson or unit of work and relinquish it for the next. The stress is on working with, not for, colleagues.

Although synergetic teams sometimes select permanent leaders for administrative purposes, the "leader" generally does not receive extra pay or privileges for accepting the assignment. In some schools, department chairmen have become members of synergetic teams and wear two hats. Administratively, they carry the burden of extra duties, while instructionally, they function as regular members of teams and share leadership with teammates during various units of work.

Synergetic teams vary in their approach from limited cooperation to complete association. For this reason, these teams are sometimes referred to as cooperative or associative teams based upon the degree of partnership the participants achieve.

HOW TEAM TEACHING IS BEING USED IN ELEMENTARY SCHOOLS

As already indicated, the teaching teams used in Lexington, Pittsburgh, and Claremont are hierarchic teams. Synergetic teams are used in other programs described here—in Shaker Heights, North Olmsted and Chagrin Falls, Ohio.

In Lexington, Massachusetts

The first elementary school team teaching program to involve a total faculty was initiated at the Franklin Elementary School in Lexington, Massachusetts, in September 1957. It was developed under the aegis of Harvard's School and University Program for Research and Development (SUPRAD) and supervised by the members of the Harvard Graduate School of Education faculty. The project, initiated as a five-year program of research and development, was conceived by Francis Keppel and Judson T. Shaplin and directed by Robert H. Anderson.

In 1961, the program was extended to the Joseph Estabrook School, one of the first elementary schools in the country to be specifically designed as a team-teaching school. The experience at Franklin served as a basis for planning the design of Estabrook.

The instructional staff at the Franklin School is organized into three hierarchic teams, called Alpha, Beta, and Omega. Team Alpha provides instruction for grades one and two, Team Beta for grades three and four, and Team Omega for grades five and six. Approximately 200 children are in each group.

In Lexington, each team has a team leader, two senior teachers, two, three, or four regular teachers, a teacher aide, and a clerical aide. In addition, special teachers are employed for art, music, and physical education.

The district director of research and development, the principal, and three team leaders constitute an administrative cabinet responsible for operational procedures. The team leader is free of instructional duties about one-third of the time in order to handle administration and supervision.

Although one of the original objectives of the program was to use the team leader position as a means of keeping outstanding teachers in the classroom, some team leaders now perceive team leadership as a stepping stone to a future administrative position.

Senior teachers in the team receive a salary differential for their superior status, but the role of the senior teacher has not yet been clearly defined. They are expected to be more expert in subject knowledge or teaching techniques, but the "merit pay" aspect of their position has always been open to question.

The teams at Lexington have been successful. But bear in mind that they have received generous grants of money and help from the Ford Foundation and Harvard University. Any school attempting to emulate this plan must be prepared to expend enormous time and energy planning, scheduling, and administering the program. When a school moves directly into a total team teaching situation, it must also be prepared to replace uncooperative or uninterested teachers with new staff members.

In Pittsburgh

In Pittsburgh, Ford Foundation grants in 1960 and 1961 led to a large-scale experiment in team teaching which now involves some 25,000 pupils. The first year, five elementary schools in a congested, downtown area participated in the experiment. In 1961, three additional elementary schools entered the program.

15

By 1965, 46 elementary schools were engaged in team teaching.

The teaching team usually consists of four regular teachers and a team leader assisted by a teacher intern and a team aide, called a "team mother" in the elementry schools (see Figure 1).[2] Units of instruction are normally introduced to the entire group

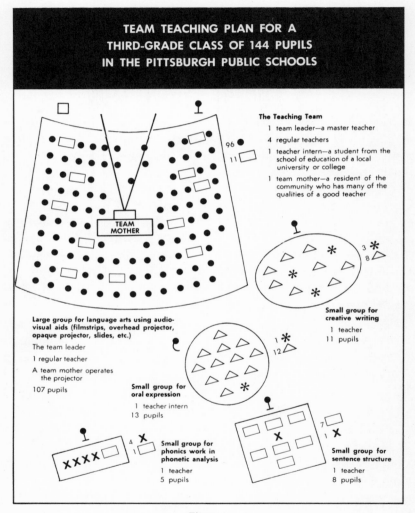

TEAM TEACHING PLAN FOR A
THIRD-GRADE CLASS OF 144 PUPILS
IN THE PITTSBURGH PUBLIC SCHOOLS

The Teaching Team

1 team leader—a master teacher

4 regular teachers

1 teacher intern—a student from the school of education of a local university or college

1 team mother—a resident of the community who has many of the qualities of a good teacher

TEAM MOTHER

Large group for language arts using audio-visual aids (filmstrips, overhead projector, opaque projector, slides, etc.)

The team leader

1 regular teacher

A team mother operates the projector

107 pupils

Small group for creative writing

1 teacher

11 pupils

Small group for oral expression

1 teacher intern

13 pupils

Small group for phonics work in phonetic analysis

1 teacher

5 pupils

Small group for sentence structure

1 teacher

8 pupils

Figure 1

---

[2] *Pupils, Patterns, and Possibilities: A Description of Team Teaching in Pittsburgh*, 1961 Annual Report of the Superintendent of Schools, p. 15.

by one teacher. Later, in small groups, the children work on special projects, research, or a review of material.

Under the Pittsburgh team teaching plan, the team leader's major responsibilities are as follows:

1. To maintain a full teaching load.
2. To call team meetings at least once a week.
3. To coordinate the program of the team.
4. To meet with the principal and other team leaders on matters of school policy, space, and equipment.
5. To set up a schedule on the basis of team decision.
6. To support the less experienced members of the team.
7. To seek supervisory support in areas of team weakness.
8. To serve as the contact person for all general information related to the team.
9. To plan the work of the teacher intern and the team mother or aide.

The intern program serves as in-service training for teacher-trainees. In 1960, 40 aspiring teachers received such training. Since that time, the number has increased to more than 400.

Weekly team meetings are held to determine the amount of large-group, small-group, and individualized or specialized instruction to be given. In the primary grades, children are in assigned homerooms and receive most of their instruction from the same homeroom teacher. However, they average more than one-fourth of their time in team teaching operations. Because of departmentalization in the intermediate grades, a different team procedure is used (see Figure 2).[3]

● *Cost of the project.* We have stated earlier that a school embarking on a hierarchic team teaching program must be prepared to meet additional expenditures. The Pittsburgh Team Teaching project is no exception. As Charles Hayes, Director of the project, has stated: "The over-all Pittsburgh Team Teaching project cost is about 15 per cent above regular per pupil costs. Excluding the compensatory education features of the Project the additional cost to Pittsburgh is about $12,200 per school. This figure includes the 10 per cent additional pay given to four team leaders and the total salary of four team mothers."[4]

However, as Hayes also points out, "The cost for team teaching . . . is considerably below the expense of a significant

---
[3] *Pupils, Patterns, and Possibilities*, p. 19.
[4] "Team Teaching in Culturally Deprived Areas," *The National Elementary Principal*, January 1965, p. 65.

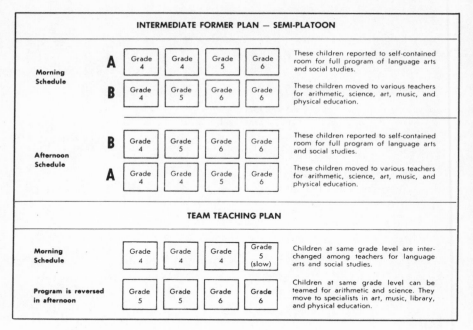

INTERMEDIATE FORMER PLAN — SEMI-PLATOON

Morning Schedule	**A**	Grade 4	Grade 4	Grade 5	Grade 6	These children reported to self-contained room for full program of language arts and social studies.
	B	Grade 4	Grade 5	Grade 6	Grade 6	These children moved to various teachers for arithmetic, science, art, music, and physical education.
Afternoon Schedule	**B**	Grade 4	Grade 5	Grade 6	Grade 6	These children reported to self-contained room for full program of language arts and social studies.
	A	Grade 4	Grade 4	Grade 5	Grade 6	These children moved to various teachers for arithmetic, science, art, music, and physical education.

TEAM TEACHING PLAN

Morning Schedule	Grade 4	Grade 4	Grade 4	Grade 5 (slow)	Children at same grade level are interchanged among teachers for language arts and social studies.
Program is reversed in afternoon	Grade 5	Grade 5	Grade 6	Grade 6	Children at same grade level can be teamed for arithmetic and science. They move to specialists in art, music, library, and physical education.

Figure 2

reduction of pupil-teacher ratio. And team teaching can, in the long run, be a more successful method of raising the level of instruction."

In California (the Claremont Plan)

In California, the Claremont Graduate School has developed a "school-within-a-school" model consisting of a group of pupils, a faculty team with five to seven teachers, an auxiliary teacher, a teacher aide, and a teaching intern. In a typical school, 20 teachers are organized into three faculty teams. An unusual feature of this plan is the use of an auxiliary teacher who serves as a substitute approximately 20 days per year. This frees team members for planning. The auxiliary teacher also acts as a substitute for team members who are absent because of illness. This provides a continuity of instruction for the team.

The teacher aide takes care of clerical and other nonteaching duties. He also acts as a monitor for large groups of students and as a tutor for individuals and small groups. In schools participating in the Claremont program, the more capable aides are encouraged to move into the teaching internship program during their second year. The intern teacher is an integral part of the team and in effect is the beneficiary of an excellent in-service training program.

The Claremont program claims 13 advantages:

1. Teachers are relieved from routine tasks.
2. Teachers are involved in the in-service training of others.
3. Teachers are responsible for curriculum development.
4. Scheduling and grouping is flexible.
5. The correlation of school work, homework, and field trips is improved.
6. Students advance at their own rates.
7. Guidance is improved.
8. Talented citizens are used.
9. Parental relationships are improved.
10. There is more regard for learning and scholarship.
11. Children receive instruction from the best qualified teacher.
12. Pupils get to know several teachers well while retaining the self-contained classroom organization.
13. Teachers get to know youngsters who will be assigned to their classes in future years.

In Shaker Heights, Ohio

Moreland Elementary School in Shaker Heights, Ohio, is an old two-story building in a radically changing neighborhood. Its dynamic principal encouraged teachers to innovate; and in 1961, the first attempts at synergetic team teaching were made.

By 1963, three second grade teachers held regularly combined classes to present films, filmstrips, and some content areas.

In the sixth grade, three teachers conducted large-group sessions approximately twice per week. Each teacher was responsible for planning lessons in his major area of strength (that is, science, language arts, and social studies). While each subject was taught in the large group, all teachers were present. Follow-up discussions were held in the regular classroom with classes divided into small groups. Making use of the services of a consultant, the principal and the faculty constantly strived to improve their procedures. They placed an increasing emphasis on flexible grouping and individualized instruction.

19

The principal kept all faculty members apprised of developments and personally attended most planning sessions. By September of 1964, the fourth and fifth grade teachers captured by the enthusiasm of their second and sixth grade colleagues, launched their own teams.

The fourth grade team of three teachers planned and taught several units such as "Animals," "Geology," "Simple Machines," and "Power and Energy." They also used a team approach in mathematics, reading, and language arts. The three fifth grade teachers began working together in health education, social studies, reading, mathematics, and science. Two units—"Sound" and "Sense Organs"—were taught as correlated lessons in health and science.

In September 1965, first and third grade teams were formed, and Moreland became a 100 percent team teaching school.

In discussing team teaching, the principal states: "The demands made on my time are great, but I love it. Meeting with team members and discussing the total instructional program represents supervision of a different type. These teachers are innovators; they are growing professionally. I thoroughly enjoy my role as a helper."

As indicated, these teachers are innovators. For example, three second grade teachers developed a unit on "Mexico." Walls were decorated with travel posters, and all three classes attended large-group presentations of films and filmstrips. A mother who had recently visited Mexico wore a native dress and showed colored slides of her trip. The music teacher taught the children Mexican songs. A Spanish speaking teacher taught an English lesson in which he pointed out the many words derived from Spanish origins. The physical education teacher, caught up in the excitement, did some library research and followed up by teaching the children how to play Mexican games. The unit culminated in a fiesta at which Mexican food was served and Mexican music was played and sung. The room was decorated with paintings of Mexico that the children had prepared during their art periods. When team members were asked if they had any major problems with the unit, they replied: "Yes, in trying to leave 'Mexico' to start the next project!"

Another unusual team effort was carried out in a fourth grade unit entitled "Impressionism." In large-group lessons, pupils were taught Haiku poetry. This simple three-line Japanese style is well suited to the interests and abilities of children. One teacher, whose love of poetry was readily transmitted to the students, used the overhead projector to illustrate the lesson (the other two teachers attended as observers). Children were shown that Haiku has five syllables on the first line, seven on the second line, and five on the third. An example was given and with the help of pupils, syllables were identified and underlined.

> All night the rag-ged
> Clouds and wind had on-ly one
> Com-pan-ion—the moon.

The teacher explained that the purpose of the poem was to create a mood. Children volunteered to explain the meaning of *mood,* and finally agreed that it was a state of mind or feeling.

At the close of the illustrated lecture, mimeographed question sheets were distributed for students to complete. Answers were then flashed on the screen, and the children corrected their own papers. In subsequent lessons, pupils discovered that poetic moods could also be expressed by means of music or art. As they listened to the strains of Debussy, they were encouraged to draw whatever they "saw" in their mind's eye. The children culminated this activity by creating Haiku poems to express the mood captured in their drawings. The team lesson correlated several subjects and capitalized on the combined talents of three teachers.

In North Olmsted, Ohio

In North Olmsted, Ohio, the population explosion led inadvertently to an improvement in staff utilization. When the Chestnut Elementary School outgrew its physical capacity, additional space was rented in a nearby church. Two teachers and their 52 second grade pupils moved into one large room. Realizing that team teaching was their only recourse, the teachers and principal began planning with the help of this writer. Cognizant of the need for small-group space, we equipped an adjoining storage room with a portable chalkboard, tables, and chairs. An overhead projector and screen were obtained for the large room.

The teachers agreed that introductory and enrichment lessons would be taught in the large room, and that each faculty member should teach areas of his strength and interest. They also agreed that the small room would be used for remedial work and discussion.

Teachers presented large-group lessons in such subjects as mathematics, social science, handwriting, spelling, and English. To illustrate such presentations, they used films, filmstrips, transparencies, and a project globe. For example, as one teacher made use of the overhead projector to demonstrate how certain letters of the alphabet were formed, the other teacher moved about the room checking seat-work and giving individual help. At the conclusion of the lesson, those children needing special attention were taken to the small room.

This small room was in frequent use. At times, it was the setting for discussion with advanced pupils; at other times, it provided a place to meet with those needing remedial attention. These teachers followed a simple rule: *help the child who needs help at the moment he needs it.*

• *Adapting physical facilities.* The advantages of this synergetic approach became apparent to others. Within a year, first and sixth grade teachers voluntarily formed teams. Because physical arrangements were different, facilities were modified. In one case, two teachers occupied a former kindergarten room. By moving clothing racks into position to form a portable, low level wall, they created a room within a room (see Figure 3).

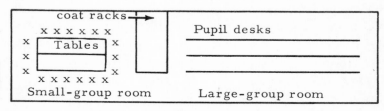

Figure 3

The sixth grade team occupied two adjoining rooms with a folding partition between. They merely opened the partition to create one large room. By moving free-standing bookshelves into position, a small-group area was formed. By putting desks one against the other, aisles were eliminated and the room became more spacious. Teachers were able to move around easily and every child had an excellent view (see Figure 4).

22

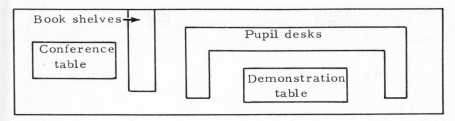

Figure 4

By 1965, ten teams in North Olmstead were using similar patterns.

In Chagrin Falls, Ohio

Using Dr. Samuel Johnson's motto "Nothing will ever be attempted if all possible objections must first be overcome," five teachers in Chagrin Falls, Ohio, are determined to succeed. These five team members of the Lewis Sands Primary School share a small building referred to as the "Little Red Schoolhouse." This annex to the main building is 60 feet by 70 feet in size, has no interior walls, and houses 110 children. Movable cabinets and curtains form partitions between learning areas.

The original team consisted of four teachers (later increased to five) selected from eight volunteers. A three-week workshop held in August, 1961, enabled team members to make final preparations for the project. During the workshop, they developed nine objectives.

1. To know each child as an individual.
2. To create an atmosphere of love and understanding.
3. To help each child learn at his own rate.
4. To guide and direct children in each skill area.
5. To help each child meet success.
6. To help children gain effective understanding of self-control and to obtain good habits of group behavior.
7. To help each child develop consideration and thoughtfulness in working.
8. To help children establish the foundations of good work habits.
9. To create an atmosphere in which learning is enjoyed.

23

After two years of experience with both first and second grade children, it was decided to continue the project with the second grade only. By 1964, a regular pattern had evolved.

• *How the project works.* Two teachers are usually on one side of the room with half the children. They operate as a small team for teaching arithmetic, social studies, and science. The 55 children meet in a variety of group sizes for these subjects. On the other side of the room, three teachers share responsibility for instruction in reading, English, and spelling. This distribution of teachers places an emphasis upon small groups in the language arts. At times, the curtain is opened for large-group instruction involving the entire 110 children. More often, instruction is repeated twice to groups of 55.

Although the teachers are pleased with results, the lack of walls, which is no problem in small teams, creates a noise factor when five groups are operating simultaneously. Although this distraction seems to diminish after teachers and children become accustomed to the "Little Red Schoolhouse," it does persist. In the future, when carpeting and an acoustical ceiling are installed, this problem will be reduced to a minimum.

According to members of this team, one of the great strengths has been "professional growth through day-to-day relationships with colleagues." This comment, in fact, is repeated by members of teams throughout the United States. Although teachers have preached cooperation, few have practiced it. Many who do, are actually surprised to find it works. When teachers help each other, the result is self-improvement and staff growth. Problems seem smaller when they are shared.

HOW TEAM TEACHING IS BEING USED IN HIGH SCHOOLS

As in elementary schools, team teaching has been introduced into high schools on a total basis, or as pilot projects in specified subject areas.

The Ridgewood High School—Innovation in Practice

In 1960, Ridgewood High School in Norridge, Illinois, went through the experience of embarking on a team teaching program. During the summer faculty members had attended a team teaching workshop, and on September 15, put their plans into action. Although the building was new, it had not been designed specifically for team teaching and had to be modified as the project moved along.

All subjects are team taught, and in some cases, teams are formed across subject lines—for example, one English teacher and one history teacher may be assigned 60 students and a double block of time. A typical instructional team consists of two to six teachers aided by interns and a clerical assistant.

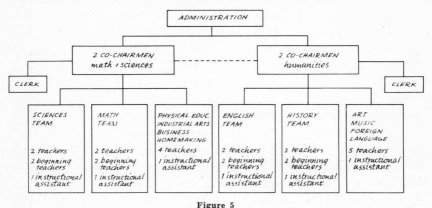

Figure 5

Team Organization, Based on Ridgewood High School (Source: Educational Facilities Laboratories, *High Schools, 1962,* New York: The Laboratories, p. 15)

As Figure 5 illustrates, teachers at Ridgewood are organized administratively into two major teams: humanities and mathematics-science. Each is subdivided into instructional teams. The humanities division includes English, history, foreign language, music, art, and business education. The team leader of mathematics-science also supervises home economics, industrial arts, and physical education.

Although a hierarchy exists, consisting of team leaders, teachers, interns, and clerks, the position of *master teacher* has not been used. The principal, Eugene Howard, has indicated that an excessively hierarchical structure might have "a deleterious effect on morale."

Planning sessions are usually held twice per week. Teachers may attend a humanities team meeting one day, an English team meeting the other. Such planning is essential to smooth operation. For example, in the mathematics-science team, it was agreed

25

to integrate health instruction into several disciplines. Information about the dangers of tobacco, alcohol, and drugs was placed in a biology unit on the central nervous system. Physiology of exercise was incorporated by the physical education teachers into a unit on the muscular system. The home economics team agreed to teach personal hygiene, grooming, and posture as part of a unit on the skin and its care. Such team planning makes use of the best qualified instructors for each phase and avoids duplication of effort.

• *Space at Ridgewood.* There are no "standard size" rooms at Ridgewood. Where you might expect to find classrooms, you discover small seminar spaces equipped with conference tables and chairs for a maximum of 15 pupils.

A divisible auditorium permits large-group instruction. When open, it can serve 830 students. With flexible walls closed, it provides space for three large groups simultaneously.

Other areas at Ridgewood are utilized for individual work. Most are equipped with study carrels for independent study. These areas hold from 30 to 50 students each. There are four English-history laboratories, a language laboratory, a business education laboratory, a music area with individual practice rooms, a small library for approximately 70 students, and a Humanities Resource Center with space for about 55.

Ridgewood's facilities for independent study would be more than ample in some schools, but are inadequate for the present program. As pupils learn good habits of study, the need for proper facilities grows. Ridgewood is now in that situation, and will soon add more space for individual work.

• *Other innovations at Ridgewood.* Although Norridge, Illinois, is a typical middle class community with only 50 percent of its students college bound, Ridgewood has the highest daily rate of library circulation and attendance of any small or medium sized school in Cook County. This is a result, no doubt, of the emphasis upon independent learning.

Ridgewood uses an electronic computer to generate the flexible schedule. The school day is built around modules of 20 minutes with a varying number of modules for each activity. The scheduled portion of each pupil's program consists of large-group instruction, laboratory work, independent study, and small group discussion. Unscheduled time is used for supervised or unsupervised study, based upon the student's degree of responsibility. Approximately 50 percent of the pupils at Ridgewood have "honors passes" which allow them to spend their unscheduled time as they see fit. Some use this time for informal "chats" in the cafeteria, but most students may be seen working or studying in laboratories, empty classrooms, or the library. Abuse of an honors pass means revocation and supervised study.

Incidentally, Mr. Howard maintains that the school's experience with the electronic computer has shown:

1. A schedule of great complexity, such as the Ridgewood schedule, can be built by computer at less over-all cost than if it were done by hand by an administrator.

2. The computer-built schedule has fewer conflicts than does the handmade schedule.

3. Class lists, room utilization lists, teacher schedules, and student schedules are extremely accurate. For a modular schedule such lists are almost impossible to develop accurately by hand except at great cost in time and money.

4. The greatest advantage to the school of a computer-built modular schedule is that the scheduler, in the process of generating his master schedule, is able to construct a large number of preliminary schedules. He can analyze each and then incorporate improvements in each succeeding run until he reaches a satisfactory and workable combinantion of courses, time allocations, teachers, and rooms within the scope the school has indicated.[5]

One of the biggest problems Ridgewood faces is how to handle visitors. Ridgewood has succeeded in "building a better mousetrap," and the world is beating a path to its door. Few new high schools in America have failed to feel its influence. Architects and educators, traditionalists and innovators, have trod its floors. Only a most unusual person could walk away from Ridgewood without seeing education in a new light.

The Nova High School—a Glimpse into the Future

In 1960, the South Florida Educational Center in Broward County embarked on a three-year effort including study, consultation, and visitation, to find the best possible organizational pattern for an educational complex that will eventually encompass all levels of instruction—kindergarten through graduate school. The first unit of this complex, the Nova High School,

---

[5] Educational Facilities Laboratories, *School Scheduling By Computer—The Story of GASP* (New York: The Laboratories, 1964), p. 11.

which opened its doors in September 1963, was designed and built for full utilization of team teaching.

Teaching teams in Nova are of the hierarchic type and make use of paraprofessional help. Using a nongraded team teaching plan, Nova keeps its groups flexible and stresses the importance of the individual. Space is provided for large-group instruction and small-group discussion, as well as for independent study. The administration is committed to the belief that team teaching provides "an environment that encourages improvement."

When you walk down the hall of Nova High School, excitement is in the air. What makes Nova new? Nova has its own television studio and closed-circuit broadcasting system. The school is air-conditioned, and all general areas are carpeted. A data processing room includes a key punch machine, sorter, microfilm camera, and reader-printer. Storage and retrieval of information is a reality. Two well-equipped lecture halls, each with a capacity of 200 students, may be divided into small classrooms by folding, sound-proof walls. In lieu of a traditional library, the school has resource centers that contain study carrels, teaching machines, tape recorders, record players, filmstrip projectors, television receivers, and microfilm readers as well as books and magazines.

Although these innovations may seem to have been designed by prodigal architects, this is not the case. Expensive, little-used facilities were eliminated. Nova has no auditorium, no spectator-size gym, no cafeteria, and no kitchen. Pupils bring lunches or eat at snack bars. A protected patio area is provided for dining and lounging. Assemblies are held outdoors or via television. The building was designed for 1,725 students and is operating at capacity 220 days per year—or, 40 days more than the national average.

The administrators realize that they have not reached Utopia, but they proudly refer to Nova as the "School of Tomorrow-Today." Its principal states, "No one knows how much and how fast a youngster can learn under ideal conditions. We aim to find out."

The Mayfield High School

In Mayfield, Ohio, Mayfield High School was designed to be flexible and functional. Basically, the school is built in the form of two cubes connected by an enclosed area containing a cafeteria and student lounge. One cube contains the academic area and the other houses the "noise" area (i.e., gym, music, shop and auditorium).

Encouraged by the superintendent and principal, two energetic department heads formed synergetic teams. These teams were developed on a voluntary basis to teach American History and American Literature. After a year of experience, it was only natural to explore the possibility of correlating the two. Within the framework of a traditional schedule, a simple procedure was devised to make this possible. Four classes, totaling 120 pupils, were scheduled as follows:

Subject:	Am. Lit.	Am. Lit.	Am. Hist.	Am. Hist.
Teacher:	A	B	C	D
Period: I	Section 1	Section 2	Section 3	Section 4
II	Section 3	Section 4	Section 1	Section 2

This schedule allowed teachers to: (1) meet in separate classes, (2) work as literature or history teams of two teachers and 60 pupils or (3) combine the entire 120 students for any portion of two consecutive hours.

Out of this beginning has grown a humanities team that has captured the interest of students and teachers alike. The art teacher delivered a series of lectures on American art and architecture. Pupils attended sessions on American music. The movie *Advise and Consent* was shown and discussed both as a literary work and a glimpse of contemporary politics. Students also attended a debate on Medicare, a panel discussion of American authors, an illustrated lecture about World War II, and sessions on "Poetry with Frank Baxter," and "Mark Twain Tonight." These combined classes not only saved the time and energy of teachers, but raised the cultural outlook of pupils. They learned that history is more than a series of political maneuvers and military battles. They came to recognize how authors, painters, musicians, and poets are influenced by, and help to shape, the flow of events.

Teachers were amazed at the amount of overlap eliminated in a correlated approach. As units of work were developed, bibliographies revealed that many books had been used in more than one course. By combining efforts, teachers also saved time for other functions. For example, while two history teachers took responsibility for 120 students, the two English teachers were able to use the time advantageously for planning. Examinations for the entire group of pupils were monitored by one or two teachers, freeing others for preparation of future lessons.

When it was inconvenient for 120 students to meet, teachers resorted to the team-within-a-team method. This meant repetition to two groups of 60, but that was still better than four groups of 30. Within the subgroup of 60, one teacher took 45 to the library for independent study, while the remaining teacher held a small-group discussion with 15. Or, two small groups met in seminars simultaneously, while 30 students were supervised by the librarian.

At times, when the large-group presentation was aimed at the average student, 100 would attend, while a dozen accelerated students were excused for individual research and eight were receiving remedial instruction. It was possible for one teacher to provide tutorial help to a single pupil for as long as two hours. Flexible grouping allowed just that. Group size could vary from one student to 120 students.

The success of team teaching in the eleventh grade led to more pilot projects. With the help of this consultant, administrators and teachers had the courage to tackle a complex twelfth grade offering. Pupils had traditionally received one year of English literature and composition, one-half year of civics and one-half year of sociology. (Civics and sociology groups were exchanged at mid-year and each course was then repeated.)

To permit a coordinated approach, the social science teachers agreed to develop a one-year course combining the two subjects. To correlate literature with sociology, the English teachers developed a course in world literature. Units of sociology and world literature were then scheduled to coincide. When the social science teachers moved into chapters based upon civics, the English teachers then presented linguistics and composition. Thus, at times, teachers functioned in two separate teams. However, planning was continued on a joint basis so the fusion into a team of four could occur at the appropriate time. As before, art and music teachers supplemented their efforts. The addition of a student teacher from a local university increased the flexibility of the team. Instead of being thrust into the "sink or swim" pool of the self-contained room, this student teacher absorbed knowledge and techniques from four experienced teachers and rapidly developed into a fully qualified member of the team.

This unique twelfth grade humanities approach began with a unit entitled "Who Am I?" Using anthropology, sociology and literature, students traced their origins and learned about the influence of Greek thought upon Western man. They studied the Greek philosophers, writers, and historians. They were introduced to Greek sculpture and architecture. With fascination they learned about the impact of Greek teachers upon their Roman masters. Roman civilization was studied in a similar vein. Culture was seen to be part of history, and history came to life.

Could one teacher, working in isolation, develop and teach such a course? When this question was discussed with Dr. Bernard Knox, director of the Center for Hellenic Studies in Washington, D.C., he stated: "Even at the university level, if such a man exists, I don't know him. It is an effort for any expert to keep up with a single field. It would be almost impossible to be an expert in literature, history, art and music."

Dr. Harold Clark, the economist, would heartily agree. In discussing specialization, he said: "They now publish over 6,000 books per year in the field of economics alone. If I were to read 10 per day, I couldn't keep up and I still haven't learned to read 10 books per day."

The Brecksville High School

If teachers are to stay abreast of new information, they must reject the idea they are the fountain of all wisdom. When pupils are restricted to the limits of the teacher's knowledge, learning becomes a prison.

Recognizing this fact, five teachers in Brecksville, Ohio, developed a synergetic team within an otherwise traditional program. Previously they taught 650 students in 28 sections of tenth grade world history, eleventh grade American history, and twelfth grade American government. Each teacher taught his subject as often as five times per day.

By rescheduling and pooling their talents, they now teach approximately 125 students per period. No subject is offered more than twice a day. Students meet in the lecture hall for large-group presentations two or three times per week. One day each week is reserved for small-group discussion in groups of 15 or fewer students. The remaining time is spent on independent study in the library.

Instructors use the overhead projector and a series of well-prepared transparencies to illustrate each lecture. Presentations are taped or mimeographed and are made available for absentees or for review.

In a lesson on the Peloponnesian War, the instructor explained the background of Sparta and Athens, the causes and results of their conflict. Pupils received a sheet containing thought-provoking questions, a vocabulary list, and a short bibliography of supplementary readings for independent study. In small-group sessions during the week, students discussed the confrontation between Sparta and Athens and the implications for today. They were not memorizing names and dates, they were thinking about causes and effects. They learned that history has written a message for men who can read.

According to the principal of Brecksville High School, the enthusiasm generated by the teachers "rubs off on the student so much so that parents tells us their children are discussing history at the dinner table."

The teachers, too, were enthusiastic about what they were doing. They said: "The team teaching approach allowed us to develop subjects in depth." One team member maintained he had never put as much time into preparation before entering the team. He stated: "Let's face it, when you get up in front of 125 students and some colleagues, you had better be prepared." Another teacher, new to the profession, said, "It's marvelous! I had an opportunity to work with four experienced teachers and their help has been invaluable." This attitude is universal.

IMPLEMENTING A TEAM TEACHING PROGRAM

A successful team teaching program depends more on people than upon the purse, more on faculties than upon facilities. One may find dormant programs in schools "designed for team teaching" and dynamic programs in archaic buildings. Invariably, administrative leadership and careful planning are the keys to success. The principal who believes he can sit in his office and shuffle papers while teachers dream up new ideas, is suffering a delusion. As educational reports repeatedly state, *reform must be instituted by administrators*. Hammering home this point, a New York State report said: "Contrary to general opinion, teachers are not change agents for instructional innovations of major scope." Perhaps this explains why educational progress has been so slow. More principals should provide the necessary leadership.

Begin by Improving Faculty Meetings

As many administrators know, typical faculty meetings are frequently a waste of everyone's time. Teachers are often treated as functional illiterates. Rules and regulations that could be just as easily put into writing are read aloud. Precious hours are spent discussing "The Flower Fund" or other bits of equally unimportant administrivia.

If you are about to embark upon a truly innovative program, you must use such time for *dynamic* meetings. Encourage teachers to examine—and with an objective eye—the school's educational program. Make comparisons, not with what education is, but with what it ought to be. See that teachers explore, report on, and discuss new curricular ideas and teaching methods. When they become aware of weaknesses in the traditional program and recognize that you sincerely desire change, some will invariably volunteer to try a new approach. When this occurs, join them enthusiastically in cooperative, democratic planning.

Initiate Constructive Planning Sessions

Through active participation, you can help to build the harmonious interpersonal relationships so essential to the operation of a successful school. Be careful, however, to avoid dominating planning sessions. When the social climate is characterized by tension or submission, teachers are unlikely to have sufficient motivation to contribute constructively. On the other hand, in schools where administrators and teachers operate in partnership, the levels of instruction and morale are usually high.

Keep in mind that planning sessions are essential to success and that they must be regularly scheduled. Limited to his own ingenuity, a teacher often runs dry. Encouraged and stimulated by colleagues, he remains creative. As a wise father once said to his son, "If we each have a dollar bill and trade, we each still

33

have one dollar. But if we each have an idea and trade, we each have two ideas."

Getting a Program Underway

An over-anxious administrator cannot launch a successful program through administrative fiat. Success comes about through changes in teachers' attitudes and through a growth in understanding, not through duress. When properly led, many teachers are willing to try team teaching; when pushed, most resist. Invariably, team teaching succeeds on a voluntary basis, but fails when imposed on unwilling or uncooperative teachers.

Conversely, an over-cautious administrator cannot develop a successful team if he insists on waiting for an abundance of funds or facilities. He should be willing to begin with as few as two team members in a single subject. If the first effort is carried out successfully by enthusiastic teachers, other courses and other teachers may be added in time.

EXAMPLES:

At Lutheran High School West, two teachers developed a synergetic team for the teaching of American history. During a single daily period, they met with 58 students in the school cafeteria. With the use of an overhead projector and portable screen, this room became a lecture hall. For discussion, pupils gathered around cafeteria tables in opposite corners of the room. Students engaged in independent study had ready access to an adjoining library. The cafeteria-library combination provided an excellent team teaching area and freed two critically needed classrooms. This initial project was closely watched from the time of its inception. Its success led to the formation of comparable teams in Lutheran High School East on the opposite side of Cleveland.

Using a similar approach, Freemont High School, Sunnyvale, California, began its project with two social studies teachers "teamed" in a course entitled "Senior Problems." From this inauspicious beginning in 1959, team teaching has spread throughout the building, a flexible schedule has been adopted, and the school is engaged in a program of total improvement.

Planning for Facilities and Equipment

Although some buildings severely handicap the development of teams, the imaginative principal will find new uses for old facilities. For example, if no specifically designed space is available for large-group instruction, have your teams use one of the following: auditorium, little theater, multi-purpose room, cafeteria, band room, choral room, study hall, or school lobby. When no suitable space is available, some schools have removed walls between rooms.

Fortunately, space and equipment for small-group discussion poses no problem. The only requirement is that students be able to engage in face-to-face discussion. Classrooms, library conference rooms, and cafeterias have all proven excellent. Although it is advantageous to work with only one small group at a time, many teachers have found that they can easily supervise two groups within the same or adjoining rooms. This, of course, depends upon the rapport established between teacher and pupils.

You may find space for independent study difficult to locate. Libraries in secondary schools are often inadequate and in elementary schools frequently nonexistent. In such schools, teams frequently improvise by using some classrooms for independent study while other classrooms are used for small-group discussion. By adding reference shelves, book trucks, tapes and records, earphones, filmstrip viewers, and other media, you can make such a plan feasible.

Also, when planning a team approach, see that your building is equipped with a thermographic or diazo copier for making transparencies and at least one overhead projector. This modern teaching tool has become indispensable for large-group instruction. Furthermore place the projector in the large-group area and leave it there. This is more advantageous than having teams check it in and out of an audiovisual room. When a projector is easily accessible, it is more likely to be used.

• *Using old facilities successfully.* In Mayfield, Ohio, a junior high principal is proving that a new program can be implemented in an old building. When his teachers were ready to start teaching in teams, a small gym, out of use for several years, was reopened and equipped with more than 100 folding chairs, an overhead projector, and screen for use with large groups. Tablet arm attachments were placed on the folding chairs so that students could take notes more conveniently.

The idea first began when his staff became aware of the Mayfield High School team teaching project, previously described. His teachers discussed the high school program in faculty meetings, and a number of interested teachers visited and observed the program in action. Although the high school teams were in the

35

fields of English, history, and the humanities, four junior high science teachers were intrigued by the techniques. They felt the method could be adapted to teaching biology. The principal encouraged this interest and joined them in the planning. The schedule was reworked to organize four classes of 80 to 100 pupils.

Teachers developed a course outline, agreed upon responsibilities, and wrote tentative lesson plans for several units of work. They then discussed, revised, and prepared these plans in final form. As the semester progressed, they prepared new units of work in detail and tentatively planned subsequent units. This procedure allowed for change as experience was gained.

Lectures were prepared to include enrichment material as well as basic concepts. The lecturer also had the responsibility of providing pupils with seminar questions for discussion and with suggested assignments for independent study. Team members agreed that assignments need "to be stimulating, thought-provoking, and well planned. Busy work defeats our objectives and should never be included."

A weekly schedule was distributed to each student so he could plan in advance. Even the absentee was able to keep up with his work. The schedule included dates and times for lectures, seminars, independent study, laboratory work, and examinations. Seminars and independent study were normally scheduled at the same time for different groups. While three teachers observed small-group discussion, one teacher was in the library with the remaining students working individually with those who needed help.

Through careful planning, guidance, and supervision, the principal was able to insure the success of his first team. He made teachers feel comfortable about mistakes and gave team members a free hand to try new ideas as long as thought preceded effort.

Because the faculty was kept informed about this pilot project, interest generated among other members of the staff. Two English teachers combined classes for an experiment with communications techniques and were amazed to discover what pupils could accomplish when properly motivated. Two of their boys, while working on individualized projects, wrote a "History of Music." Using an organ to demonstrate beat, tempo, and style, they traced the development of classical, semiclassical, and popular music. Fascinated with the depth and quality of the performance, the teachers arranged for the entire school to hear the program. By means of music and commentary, these boys gave a new cultural insight to all of their schoolmates. The boys, previously considered "poor" students, indicated it was their most rewarding school experience.

As a result of this experiment, the teachers were encouraged to expand their efforts. They combined other classes for large-group instruction and made their first attempt at flexible grouping. By September 1965, these English teachers were able to inaugurate a team teaching program for all 10 of their classes.

• *Turning liabilities into assets*. When the St. Edward High School in Lakewood, Ohio, was overcrowded, a number of faculty members agreed to try a form of team teaching. For example, two English and two history teachers fitted their four classes into one large and two small rooms. On one day, the two history classes were combined in the large room, while the two English classes met in the smaller rooms. The following day the procedure was reversed.

As an outgrowth of this initial effort, a major addition to the school plant was designed to include a materials preparation center, three amphitheater-type large-group instruction rooms, and an instructional materials center. The preparation center contains facilities for preparing audiovisual aids and houses a tape, film, and record library for teachers. The center also is wired for closed-circuit television broadcasting and includes a videotape recorder. Two of the large-group rooms seat 90 pupils and the third, 144. Since the rooms are fan-shaped, no student is seated more than 32 feet from the screen. The teacher can operate equipment by remote control, and has a choice of standard or rear view projection. The instructional materials center contains a library of books, films, and tapes; a team planning room; and study carrels for students. The addition is air-conditioned, and special areas are carpeted.

All of these facilities, designed to augment the team teaching program, permit experienced teachers to share their ability with a greater proportion of the student body. St. Edward is one of the few Catholic schools in America to have such an advanced educational plant; and, it all began when four classes had to be squeezed into three rooms.

37

• *Providing for flexibility.* Schools built today should be designed to provide for more efficient utilization—and for flexibility of space and equipment. In spite of great advances in school construction, many designers still cling to anachronistic ideas. For example, new schools are being built with stage facilities in the gym, which is in almost constant use during school hours and seldom available for plays, films or lectures. If it is used for PTA meetings or other assemblies in the evening, chairs must be hauled in and later removed. Gym floors are often ruined.

In the same building, one frequently finds a cafeteria standing empty a major portion of the day. With proper planning, this could have been designed as a cafetorium. In such a room, chairs and tables are already in position for meetings, and the space is available for large-group instruction or small-group discussion most of the day. In the John F. Kennedy High School at Wheaton, Maryland, operable walls are used to divide the space in a large cafeteria into two or more rooms. Kennedy High also has a divisible auditorium, similar to those at Norridge, Illinois, and at Boulder City, Nevada. Such divisible space provides for several large groups simultaneously.

Even in old buildings, flexibility may be obtained through remodeling. If a wall is removed between two rooms, each housing 30 pupils, the new space will easily accommodate 90 for large-group instruction. Similarly, a single classroom for 30, when divided into three small-group conference rooms, will hold 45 pupils. A library, equipped with study carrels, will certainly house the same number of students as comfortably as more conventional rooms.

Provide for Flexibility of Time

Just as space can be used in new ways, so can time. Although excellent team programs may operate within the confines of a traditional schedule, many educators question the need for teaching every subject five times per week for the same number of minutes. To vary time, they have turned to flexible scheduling. Most popular is the 15-minute module. Pupils may meet in the language laboratory or lecture hall for 30 minutes, in English for 45, in the gym for 60 or in lab for 75 or 90. Any multiple of 15 minutes may be used and many classes meet only two, three, or four times per week. In large schools, complicated schedules are easily handled by means of computers, as has already been explained in connection with the program at Norridge, Illinois.

There is also a trend to the "block of time" schedule. In the Middle School of Kirtland, Ohio, simplicity was the goal. As consultant to the superintendent and principal, I designed a schedule for this school under which each pupil attends four 85-minute "block of time" classes per day: (1) Math—Science, (2) English —Social Science, (3) Basic Skills—Physical Education, and (4) Unified Arts. (See Figure 6.)

KIRTLAND MIDDLE SCHOOL, KIRTLAND, OHIO: BLOCK SCHEDULE

Period	Grade: Time	6		7		8	
I.	8:00	English	S. S.	Music	Art Home Ec. Shop	Math	Science
II.		S. S.	English	Art Home Ec. Shop	Music	Science	Math
III.	9:25	Gym	Basic Skills	Math	Science	English	S. S.
IV.		Basic Skills	Gym	Science	Math	S. S.	English
V.	10:50	Music	Art Home Ec. Shop	English	S. S.	Gym	Basic Skills
VI.		Art Home Ec. Shop	Music	S. S.	English	Basic Skills	Gym
A	12:15	Lunch A			Activity Period		
B	12:40	Activity Period			Lunch B		
HR	1:05	Home Room					
VII.	1:20	Math	Science	Gym	Basic Skills	Music	Art Home Ec. Shop
VIII.		Science	Math	Basic Skills	Gym	Art Home Ec. Shop	Music
END	2:45						

Figure 6

Each teacher instructs three blocks per day and is free the other 85 minutes for team planning. Study hall, and other duties, have been eliminated. For example, in the English-Social Science block of time, teachers operate as a team of four or as two teams of two depending upon the unit being presented. Normally each team of two operates separately with 60 pupils in double-size classrooms divided by folding doors. Children change subjects at the end of 40 minutes. However, teachers may retain their groups for the entire 85 minutes or assemble the total group of 120 students in the cafeteria for any portion of the time block.

Unified Arts is taught by one teacher each in music, art, home economics, and shop. They work together as a team of two, three, or four according to need. In addition to their own facilities, they can use the cafeteria for large-group instruction, and the library for independent study.

Regardless of how a school is scheduled, whether simple or complex, the important thing to remember is to make the schedule fit your program, not the program fit your schedule.

Help the Team

Team teaching is not easy. In fact, it makes considerable demands on teachers. This is especially true initially, when members of the team need time for planning (1) to develop techniques and materials for large-group instruction, small-group discussion, and independent study, (2) to develop audiovisual aids, and (3) to prepare presentations.

Though these pressures gradually diminish as initial plans and problems are worked out, the school administration should, if possible, provide teaching teams with supporting assistance. Aides who provide teachers with help on nonprofessional tasks are referred to by a variety of titles.

• *Salaried aids.* In Lexington, Massachusetts, whose hierarchic teaching teams are complex, each team is served by a clerical aide and a teacher aide. The former is involved with "stationery-stationary" supporting tasks—that is, those performed on paper at a fixed station. The latter takes on supporting tasks demanding mobility and interaction with pupils, such as corridor, lunchroom, and bus duty. They also operate mechanical aids in the classroom, check attendance, and grade papers. Their roles, plus those of other members of Lexington's teaching teams, are described in Bair and Woodward's book, listed at the end of this booklet.

In some communities, teachers have accepted a small increase in the pupil-teacher ratio in order to offset the additional cost of a clerk. In schools where such assistance cannot be provided, teachers can still improve the situation through a division of labor. One might handle all typing for the team, another the preparation of transparencies or mimeographing.

Retired teachers are well-suited for the role of teacher aides. They are trained to work with children, enjoy the opportunity to continue their association with other teachers, usually can use the funds, and often are interested in a part-time position. Frequently the best prospects for school aides with clerical skills are married women, many of whom are mothers of children attending the school. In fact, Pittsburgh's teacher aides in the elementary school—called team mothers—must be members of the community served by the school to which they are appointed. One reason mothers find such work attractive is that they can be at home during vacations and after school hours.

- *Volunteer mothers.* At the Moreland Elementary School in Shaker Heights, Ohio, the approach is somewhat unique. Team mothers, who are all volunteers, work at the school on a mutually satisfactory schedule.

They are banded together in a group called "Team Mother Specialists, Inc." The mothers who report to the school on a given day comprise a team that includes teacher-helpers who can type, mimeograph, make transparencies, work in the library, distribute supplies, or operate audiovisual equipment. A succession of mother teams provides continuous help for teachers at no cost to the school system.

- *Student teachers.* Many teaching teams, for example, those in Pittsburgh and in the Claremont program, have found student teachers or teaching interns to be an asset. They may be assigned to teach small groups, to act as resource persons for independent study, or to present large-group instruction. As the student teacher gains proficiency, he is able to assume an increasing amount of responsibility within the team.

Pittsburgh's intern members of the teaching team usually serve with the team all day, every day, for a full semester. The intern starts by observing under the direction of the team leader. As soon as he is ready to assume some teaching responsibility, he begins to work with small remedial groups. Later he takes over classes of normal size, and may even present a large-group lesson.

41

"By the end of the semester," says project director Charles Hayes, "the service provided by most of these young people is almost equivalent to that of an additional teacher on each team." [6]

As these examples demonstrate, an ingenious principal can find many ways to provide help for his teams. In addition, his personal aid in solving problems of scheduling, room utilization and intrastaff relations can be invaluable. Although the team must rapidly learn to rely on its own resources, excessive responsibility thrust too suddenly upon team members could lead to antagonism or frustration.

Supervise the Team

A principal must also be wary of success. Once teachers are secure, they may lapse into a comfortable routine and fall far short of their potential.

Even though the program may appear to be operating successfully, you will need to observe some of its aspects such as the use being made of large-group instruction, small-group discussion, and independent study (the next section gives detail on how to plan for these three phases of team teaching). Use both praise and constructive criticism to improve team operations.

For example, because large-group instruction is similar to traditional classroom teaching, many teachers tend to overemphasize this method. Presentations may get too long, particularly in the secondary school. Lectures should normally be held to 30 minutes or less, and time should always be allowed for questions immediately after the summary. The principal will also need to be careful that large-group instruction is not used more than 30 or 40 percent of the time.

Because teachers tend to dominate discussion, check the small-groups frequently. If teachers are talking too much, this indicates a need for more in-service training. All staff members, whether in teams or not, should be familiar with group dynamics techniques, inductive teaching, and the discovery method.

Also observe independent study. Indolent or inconsiderate teachers may use the library or instructional materials center as a "dumping ground." Much of the value is lost if teachers are not available to help pupils. This phase of team teaching gives the

---

[6] "Team Teaching in Culturally Deprived Areas," *National Elementary Principal*, January 1965, p. 63.

teacher an opportunity to work with a single student or with a few. By giving individual attention, the teacher can encourage the discouraged and spur the inspired.

Keep Parents and the Community Informed

If you keep knowledgeable about team plans and progress, you will find such information extremely valuable in handling public relations. Parents are reluctant to allow anyone to *experiment* with their most precious possession. The very word *experiment* is anathema to most parents and should not be used publicly by administrators or teachers.

As already stressed, team teaching is no longer experimental. It has been proved and is functioning in hundreds of America's finest schools. A pilot team teaching project is new to the teachers involved, but it is merely the implementation of a proven, modern instructional method. It is no more to be feared by a sensible parent than the adoption of an improved curriculum. Parents want the best for their children and are pleased when they realize teachers are striving to improve. Experience shows that if administrators and teachers plan carefully and present their ideas logically, they will find an intelligent public applauding their efforts.

Orville J. Jenkins of the Shaker Heights' Moreland School is more than a dynamic principal. He uses a comprehensive grasp of public relations possibilities, a bit of showmanship, and untiring effort to inform the community about his 100 percent team teaching school.

• At "Education Parties," held in homes, a teaching team appears to discuss any phase of the school's program. The school has developed color slides, some with taped narration, for use by the teams or by community groups.

• At a recent two-night open house, children in the first three grades and their parents saw a showing of *The Moreland Story*, a 27-minute, 8mm motion picture produced to show the school's team teaching program, flexible grouping, and creative learning techniques. The second night for upper elementary students and their parents also featured the film.

• Moreland's "Team Mother Specialists" are "tremendous

PR agents," says Principal Jenkins. "They carry out into the community much more school news than we could possibly send out."

- Details about the Moreland program appear frequently in the Cleveland metropolitan press and are supplemented by *The Principal's Newsletter,* a 10-page bulletin put out by the PTA five times a year, which goes to parents and area leaders.

Envision Improved Instruction Rather than Cost Savings

Although team teaching originally was considered a means for saving money, this proved to be a fallacy. Schools developing a team teaching program often increase expenditures for summer workshops and in-service education. They frequently spend money for consultant service and travel expenses. Some spend for clerical help and teacher aides. They usually spend more for audiovisual equipment and instructional materials. Some spend to remodel rooms for large-group instruction and to develop instructional materials centers. As independent study skills improve, library circulation increases, and more is spent for books. Even in new schools designed for team teaching, money saved on construction costs is usually plowed back to provide better equipment.

Although many skillful principals have managed to develop successful team teaching programs without increasing their budgets, you will be wise to anticipate increased expenditures rather than substantial savings. Money does not guarantee good education, but good education costs money.

PLANNING FOR LARGE-GROUP INSTRUCTION, SMALL-GROUP DISCUSSION, AND INDEPENDENT STUDY

We know children learn from teachers, by themselves, and from each other. In examining these three processes, many team teachers have found a basic way to plan lessons. They study the curriculum, develop objectives, determine essential ideas to be taught and then answer three questions:

- What can students learn best from explanations by others?

- What can students learn by interaction between themselves and their teachers?

- What can students learn by themselves?

The answer to the first question suggests large-group instruction; to the second, small-group discussion; and to the third, independent study. If these three phases of the team teaching process are to be used effectively, the principal and his teachers must plan carefully.

In spite of evidence and experience to the contrary, too many teachers still insist that all teaching must be conducted in standard classrooms with equal size groups—and are apparently convinced that teaching cannot improve unless class size is reduced. Those teaching 40 pupils say 35 would be far better. Those with 35 insist 30 would be perfect. In more favored communities, those with 30 say they could really teach if only they had classes of 25. Through such empirical evidence, it seems that perfect class size is five less than whatever the teacher has now!

The conventional class of 30 pupils has proven to be the wrong size for most activities. It is inefficient for large-group instruction and ineffective for small-group discussion.

Within the team framework, flexibility is the keynote. Teachers vary the size and structure of the group, the allocation of time, and the method of instruction to be used. When team teaching is properly conducted, it provides a balanced program of (1) large-group instruction where material is visualized rather than verbalized, (2) small-group discussion where ideas are expounded and explored, and (3) independent study where the emphasis is on research rather than rote.

Using Large-Group Instruction

J. Lloyd Trump, associate secretary of the National Association of Secondary-School Principals, recently reported that teachers nationally spend an average of 46 percent of their time engaged in activities that could be done more efficiently in large groups. Working in teams, teachers are able to plan for successful large-group instruction.

● *To improve lecture presentations.* Typical teachers in conventional classes spend a tremendous amount of time talking at children. Most fail to realize they are delivering unprepared, unillustrated, low-quality lectures. Unplanned classroom talk is a poor substitute for a planned and illustrated lecture. Team teaching does more than provide the teacher time to prepare ade-

45

quately. It also motivates psychologically. A teacher is inclined to prepare exceptionally well for a presentation before a large group, especially when the group may include some interested colleagues.

Today, making use of modern media, teachers are overcoming the disadvantages and capitalizing on the advantages of the lecture method.

EXAMPLES:

> Recently, a sister at Magnificat High School in Rocky River, Ohio, gave an introduction to *Hamlet* before four combined classes of girls. It was so beautifully done that students were moved to applause.

> At Moreland Elementary School in Shaker Heights, Ohio, three classes assembled for a lesson on poetry under an exceptionally well qualified teacher who used an overhead projector in her demonstration. The children learned easily and quickly to write their own poems in free verse. The teacher shared her knowledge and love of poetry with a wide range of students and with her two colleagues.

Both of these examples were lectures. The former was compact, concise, and uninterrupted. The latter was more informal and punctuated with questions. Techniques varied, but principles were the same. Both teachers established rapport with the pupils, made a smooth transition into the body of the lecture, and later moved directly into the summary. Both kept presentations short and used visual aids. In each case, the lecture motivated children to think and do.

Properly used, the lecture is excellent for basic orientation, motivation, and enrichment. It can be employed to present many ideas in a short period of time. It assures an orderly and coherent presentation in contrast to the digressions normally found in the traditional classroom. The lecture may be profitably employed to prepare students for demonstrations, independent study, or small-group discussion. It can be used to encourage attention, to teach note taking and outlining, to arouse curiosity, to stimulate inquiry and to develop imagination and creativity.

• *To make the introduction of technical aids economically feasible.* It is now recognized that pupils can see a film, listen to an orchestra, watch a television broadcast, or listen to a speech in groups of varying size, some of which may be quite large. Many enriching experiences actually may be improved when the presentation is to large groups.

Films, tape recordings, television, and guest speakers should be utilized not only when they can supplement the teacher's presentation, but also when they can do the job better than the teacher. Every teacher should realize that he need not spend time teaching anything that can be taught better by other means.

For example, films make literature come to life, filmstrips take children to other lands, tapes transport them back through time, television brings the world into the classroom, and guest speakers lend variety. Important persons in the community who normally hesitate to prepare a presentation for 30 children often welcome the opportunity to talk with 100.

• *To save teacher time.* Obviously, large-group instruction should be planned to make more effective use of teacher time, energy, and competencies. Doing so is the very essence of large-group instruction. Time and energy are saved if a teacher gives one presentation to five groups of 30 students simultaneously. Since each presentation can be given by the best qualified member of the team, large-group instruction uses the abilities of outstanding teachers more fully.

Similarly there is little reason to test in groups of 30. Two, three, or four classes may be combined for test purposes in a library, cafeteria, or auditorium. Since it doesn't take a college degree to monitor an examination, a teacher aide can do so, freeing the teachers on the team for study, planning, or other professional use of their time.

• *To teach children to listen, to take notes, and to behave.* In the conventional classroom, the teacher follows an unpredictable pattern. If his students do not respond as he wishes to an *ad lib* lecture, he may suddenly subdue his restless charges with a difficult assignment or exam. In this mental milieu, neither the pupil nor the teacher knows what may happen next.

In contrast, students taught by teams generally have their assignments in advance. When they enter the large-group room, they expect to hear a lecture, see a film, or take a test. Whatever the situation, they are prepared. They have the proper "mind set." If the large-group presentation is more carefully prepared and more interesting than the conventional classroom presentation (as it should be), the children's curiosity and love of learning are enhanced.

47

Good results cannot be derived, however, from merely gathering children together in large groups. Pupils must be taught how to learn. Most teams present lessons early in the year on such topics as listening, studying, note taking, and outlining. A three-year Ford Foundation study at Lomond and Ludlow elementary schools in Shaker Heights, Ohio, has indicated that listening and studying skills can be greatly improved through such instruction combined with proper follow-up.

Surprisingly, experience has shown that disciplinary problems tend to disappear in the large group. Some teachers feel this is due to the presence of more than one teacher in the room. While one is concentrating on the presentation, the other takes care of attendance, tardiness, deportment, and other such details. A few psychologists feel improved behavior is the result of "mind set." They maintain that pupils generally conform when they know the behavioral limits.

Using Small-Group Discussion

Small-group discussion tests the effectiveness of any team teaching program. If students have been properly motivated to look, listen, read and think, they will relish the opportunity to express their ideas. Most pupils find it necessary not only to inhale the English language, but also to exhale it. Discussion in small groups improves personal relations among students, promotes problem solving, and develops more effective communication skills.

Small-group discussion does not mean an oral quiz conducted by a teacher in the traditional class of 30. When discussion is successful, all students in the group are closely involved in a free exchange of ideas. Such interaction cannot effectively take place within the conventional class of 30 students. Experience in hundreds of schools, backed up by evidence in the field of group dynamics, indicates the maximum size for small-group discussion is fifteen.

When a teacher listens to such a group, he is able to analyze students' reactions to course content and to assess their knowledge of it. He can observe the ability of each individual to handle data and to solve problems. From the small group, he will obtain insights that should lead to improved large-group presentations and to more effective independent study. In the small group,

48

the teacher can begin to evaluate the effectiveness of his own teaching.

• *Involve all the children.* To understand the advantage of the small group, it might be worthwhile to examine human nature for a moment. Nature has endowed human beings with a certain degree of self-centeredness. We can see evidence of this every day. The child looking at a group photograph always hunts for his own picture first. The business man looking at market quotations immediately checks to see how his stocks are doing. Boys and girls are usually more interested in their own achievements than in the success of others.

To capitalize on this natural attitude, teachers should find ways to involve each youngster in the learning process. Each should be encouraged to express his ideas. Sitting in a room where the teacher expounds is not enough. Answering an occasional question can hardly be labeled "involvement." Every child must be given the feeling that his ideas have merit, that he has personal worth. An effort should be made to see that each child has at least one successful experience daily.

• *Use the teacher as consultant-advisor.* The teacher's role in small-group discussion should be that of consultant-advisor. In this role, he may have to clarify issues and correct erroneous information, but even this function should gradually diminish as pupils gain proficiency. In time, the teacher should find himself more of an observer and counselor. When a group discussion gets lively, the teacher may become so interested that it will be all he can do to refrain from participating. But, his job is to provide educational problems and learning experiences—not to be an active participant in the discussion.

• *Provide appropriate space.* Since informality is vital to interaction, the group should be seated around a conference table or at desks arranged in a circle. Sitting in rows, staring at the backs of necks, is not conducive to discussion.

Although it is preferable to have only one small group in a classroom, two can function effectively. Portable barriers such as chalkboards, bulletin boards, or bookcases may be used to create a feeling of privacy for each group.

In some schools, teachers take pupils to the cafeteria where several discussion groups can meet simultaneously without disturbance. Although an inexperienced observer may find the noise level disturbing, the pupil participants are seldom distracted, for they are concentrating on their own discussion. It is much like a lunch meeting in a public restaurant where one converses with those in his own group and tunes out others at surrounding tables.

• *Teach children to discuss.* The physical adjustment to small-group discussion is easy. The difficulty is psychological. After years of traditional instruction, students in the small group often sit back and wait for the teacher to talk. Too often, the teacher obliges and ends up instructing a group of 10 to 15 pupils in the same manner as a group of 30. On the other hand, the teacher may resist the temptation, tell the students to discuss, and then give up because "the children just don't know how to act in a small group." The latter statement is correct; the children don't! They must learn how to discuss. This process may take several weeks or even months, but once learned it is well worth the effort.

Teachers who accept the challenge are able to capitalize on the tremendous advantage offered by the small group. They learn what pupils are really thinking. They find out who is reading and what is retained. They discover which ideas stimulate and which only stupefy. They find new ways to bring out the introvert and to control the extrovert. They note those who think before speaking and those who speak before thinking. Small-group discussion gives teachers the opportunity to know students as never before and provides a wealth of material for individual conferences.

From small-group discussions, which improve interpersonal relations and foster human dignity, a child gains valuable experiences and insights. He learns respect for another's point of view. He learns that his own ideas must be presented for review in the court of public opinion. He not only acquires pertinent information, but is a participant in a process that tends to preserve and strengthen democracy. Although each student has complete freedom to express his thoughts, he soon learns that not all talk is good talk—that lack of preparation, ignorance of facts, or irrational remarks will affect his status in the group. A worthwhile contribution, on the other hand, is readily recognized by all and tends to encourage each to do his best.

● *Use student leaders.* Experience has shown that small groups cannot function without some direction. Therefore, student leaders should be elected or appointed. Under the guidance of capable teachers, their roles can be an excellent means of developing potential leaders.

Without dominating, the group leader must maintain order, encourage pupils to talk one at a time, involve as many persons as possible in the discussion, allow minority opinions to be heard, and keep the discussion within bounds of topic and time. Rules of politeness rather than parliamentary procedure should govern. An effective discussion leader does not offer opinions or give answers, but encourages the group to develop their own thoughts. Many teachers find it advisable to provide discussion leaders with a set of questions. Leaders should realize such questions are designed to stimulate discussion, not stifle it, and that all questions need not be covered.

Another student role is that of recorder. He keeps a record of the discussion and may be called upon for a report at any time. His summary at the end of a discussion period ties the session together and serves as a basis for gauging progress. His report also serves as a springboard for additional research and study. Where teachers supervise more than one discussion group simultaneously, the recorder's record is invaluable for evaluating the session.

Naturally, competent discussion leaders, efficient recorders, and effective discussants do not develop by accident. Their development takes time, planning, and patience. The amount of structure required in small-group sessions should be diminished as students become more experienced. Certainly, greater proficiency should be expected at the end of the year than at the beginning.

● *Use flexible methods and groups.* Obviously, small group methods vary from subject to subject and grade to grade. At the primary level, small groups may meet for remedial work or for enrichment. One group may be composed of those needing help with modern mathematics or reading, another may contain those working together on clay models or on a puppet show. Whether groups are homogeneously or heterogeneously formed depends entirely on the purpose. The achievement range may be narrowed for remedial work and widened for interest groups. The same is true in upper grades. Groups should be flexible and based upon need.

Occasionally, replace the small-group discussion with a debate where students choose different sides of a controversial issue. Some teachers prefer a panel-type discussion followed by questions from the group and answers by the panel. Such debates or panels may prove to be of sufficient value to warrant presentation before the large group. Another substitute is to have students report reading done during independent study sessions.

With the tremendous growth of knowledge, students can no longer turn to the teacher for every answer. They must learn to accept themselves and others, to rub shoulders with neighbors, to test intellects and insights, to understand individual differences. If small-group discussion has fulfilled its educational function, by the time students are in the twelfth grade, little structure or guidance should be necessary on the part of the teacher.

• *Relate content material to the students.* It must also be recognized that pupils are more interested in the present than in the past. Yet, much of education deals with events of long ago. Little is accomplished if pupils don't see relationships between the content and their lives. To bridge the gap of time and interest, ideas and experiences must continually be related to living, breathing people. In studying the past, we must continually ask two questions: What did it mean to them, there, then? What does it mean to us, here, now?

EXAMPLE:
When a ninth grade class was discussing a topic entitled "Heroes," a question was raised as to whether men were born to be heroes or whether their heroism was the result of circumstances. This led to a discussion of predestination versus free will. At the conclusion of the session, the group and their teacher agreed that this was worthy of more study. They decided to find out what the great philosophers thought about this question. In subsequent discussion periods, they referred to the Bible, the Koran, the beliefs of Buddhists, the works of Plato, and the writings of Jean Paul Sartre. The level of interest and discussion was equal to what one might hear in a college seminar. Once again these students proved there is no limit to the capacity of a human mind when motivated to learn.

52

Using Independent Study

Educators have long maintained that our ultimate goal in education is to make each person a thinking, life-long learner. If we really believe that each child should become increasingly responsible for his own education, then we must focus our attention in the direction of independent study.

To be effective, independent study must be a part of, not apart from, the regular program. Its emphasis should be on creative, meaningful research that will stretch and strengthen the minds of students. Properly conducted, it will help pupils grow in self-correction, self-analysis, and self-direction.

In all cases, an emphasis should be placed on individualization of learning. Mass assignments, based on a single text, tend to stifle creativity. Pupils should be encouraged to read many sources and to use a variety of materials. As Montaigne once said: "A teacher should not be continually thundering instruction into the ears of his pupil, as if he were pouring it through a funnel, but should induce him to think, to distinguish, and to find out things for himself."

• *Provide time, space, and materials.* If large-group instruction is properly handled, the students will have received information about how to study and will be motivated to learn. But boys and girls cannot acquire good habits of independent study if the school fails to provide adequate time, space, and materials. Nor should independent study be confused with traditional homework or "busy work" assignments, which cause the conscientious pupils to rebel, while the more indolent give up.

Independent study must become part of a student's basic education; and all students should be able to complete a basic education during school hours. This may mean lengthening the school day or operating more efficiently within present time allotments. In either case, facilities should be available after school hours for those with greater interests. Taking down "keep out" signs and substituting "welcome mats" cannot help but encourage interest among those pursuing individual projects.

Independent study should be conducted in an instructional materials center or modernized school library. One great need of the nation's schools is for more and better school libraries—according to the U.S. Office of Education, 53 percent of all public school have no libraries and a great many of those in existence are inadequate. Since there are fewer libraries in elementary schools than in secondary schools, the need there is particularly acute.

The traditional library, with its anachronistic arrangements, is not conducive to independent study. Its design dates back to the days when the library was considered the province of the librarian rather than the user and when the most valuable books were chained to walls and the others were guarded from potential thieves. You cannot place students around tables in face-to-face contact, which encourages discussion, and then expect them to be silent.

If your school has a traditional library, there are ways you can make it more suitable for independent study. Place free-standing bookracks about the room to break it into small areas and build rows of study carrels along the walls. These carrels will not only provide visual screening, but will enable students to move freely to the racks without disturbing others.

As soon as funds are available, you should develop an instructional materials center. In such a center, books, tapes, films, and records are readily available; space is provided for study, viewing, listening, and discussing; the librarian can provide direction when needed; and the teacher is free to meet with individuals who have moved beyond conventional goals or with those in need of remedial help.

If we are to get youth ready for the future, we shouldn't restrict them to materials of the past. Cartridge loading 8 mm film projectors can be operated by the smallest child. Hand viewers for filmstrips are enjoyed by children of every age. The tape recorder is now simple to operate and, when placed on a table with several sets of earphones, provides an inexpensive, functional listening station. Such stations are in operation at all levels of instruction—Lomond Elementary School in Shaker Heights, Ohio; Nova High School, Fort Lauderdale, Florida; and the University of Miami at Coral Gables, to name just a few. In each of the schools mentioned, interest is high and research techniques are similar. Pupils at each level use the library key, develop a bibliography, and work with all types of material whether written, visual, or auditory.

Teachers normally record their large-group presentations and make the tapes available to students during periods of independent study. These tapes enable absentees to hear what they missed and afford others a ready means of review.

Unfortunately, many of our schools cannot yet afford closed-circuit television. Those who do have such facilities employ video-tapes for independent study as well as large-group instruction. At Nova High School as many as three different programs may be fed into the instructional materials center for use by students engaged in makeup or review sessions.

In addition to space for reading, looking, and listening, we must provide areas for the preparation of visual aids. With the increasing use of the overhead projector, transparencies are indispensable for the modern instructor. At Moreland Elementary and Ridgewood High School professional assistance is provided to help students and teachers plan and prepare transparencies. Pupils at these schools are encouraged to use visual aids in their own classroom reports.

Programed learning is another resource almost untapped in our schools. Good programs, properly used, can provide many advantages. The program never loses patience. It gives immediate reinforcement when the student is correct and provides instant correction if he is wrong. Students master materials at their own rate and seem to enjoy doing so.

Programed learning also permits individualization of instruction. For example, after correcting a set of themes, an English teacher may assign different phases of programed materials to each student requiring remedial help. One may have to study clauses and phrases, another punctuation, a third verbs and adverbs, and so on. There is no need for the teacher to make everyone listen to a lesson needed by only a few. Teachers also use programed learning for enrichment or advanced study. In some schools, students take complete programed courses in subjects where no qualified instructors are available.

• *Provide the supervision desirable.* Though independent study recognizes that every student is an individual and encourages each to progress to the limit of his ability, we should not turn all students loose to drift around the building in the hope they will learn to study. Some students respond to an honors system and can be depended upon to use their time wisely. Others must be guided. The amount of supervision necessary for a given pupil may be determined only through trial and error.

Many schools find that more than 50 percent of their pupils need little or no supervision during independent study. For the remainder of the student body, supervision is necessary, but should be gradually reduced as students become more responsible.

There is no longer any question about the need for independent study. The only question is whether administrators should urge teachers to use it wisely as part of a planned program, or allow them to continue to treat study as something which takes place only in a study hall or at home.

EVALUATING THE RESULTS OF TEAM TEACHING

Although team teaching is far beyond the experimental stage, and a multitude of administrators, teachers, pupils and parents proclaim its benefits, nonsubjective data are still scarce. In fact, those searching for an across-the-board objective evaluation may be seeking the impossible. Many educators engaged in team teaching feel that a person must be involved in the process before he can give a valid opinion of its worth. They believe administrators of team teaching programs are best qualified to measure improvements in use of staff, facilities and equipment. They say team teachers are in the prime position to judge effective use of their time, energy and talent. And, they feel pupils and parents are most competent to gauge interest in school and enthusiasm for learning.

Problem of Evaluating Pupil Progress

Team teaching has proven a headache to traditional evaluators, who compare experimental groups of pupils to control groups and report change. When they try the same procedure with team teaching the measuring sticks seldom work. There are too many variables. Once teachers change methods, other reforms follow in rapid succession. Teachers re-examine textbooks, and often supplement or replace them. They discover fundamental principles are more important than a collection of facts. They find new uses for time and space. Once team teaching is under way, teachers discard or modify procedures formerly used for better and more productive ones.

When evaluators have resorted to standardized tests and compared pupils solely on this basis, the reports (and there are hundreds of them) invariably say the same thing: "Team students did as well or better than those in the traditional program." In a way, this is surprising, for standardized tests, based on recall, should favor pupils taught in conventional classes.

While evaluators anxiously try to answer the question "Do students in a team program learn more?" team teachers are concerned with the natural response "Learn more of what?" As they team teach and re-examine old methods, they discover that traditional tests forced them to teach in traditional ways. Too many pupils can name states and their capitals, but can't locate them on a map. They can recite the preamble to the Constitution, but don't know what it means. They memorize facts about the past, but can't discuss implications for today. They can recite laws of mathematics and science, but can't solve problems.

Team teachers are discovering that the emphasis for too long has been placed on memorization and regurgitation. They are learning that it is more important for a student to know *why* than to know *when*.

The skills that team teachers stress are listening habits, note taking, large-group behavior, self-expression, and the *new* 3r's— reason, research, and responsibility. Since objective tests fail to consider these skills, they must be evaluated by subjective means. Objective measurement of pupil progress will have to wait until improved testing devices are developed.

Team Teaching Is a Change Agent

If a principal is interested in an organizational pattern in which he and his teachers can identify the school's educational problems, study them, and seek solutions, he should encourage team teaching. It provides a vehicle for change, and has the advantage of introducing change through internal rather than external forces.

Aware of the tremendous potential of team teaching as an

agent for change, the superintendent of schools in Norwalk, Connecticut, said:

> . . . We had begun with redeployment as the means for more effective staff utilization. We were swept on to consideration of improved curricula, a better use of technology and plant, and improved pupil personnel services. Team Teaching shook the entire educational web and led directly to the development of plans for a Norwalk School Improvement Program.[7]

Although readily admitting that its program had deficiencies and that many problems remained to be solved, Norwalk claimed that the program had resulted in improvements in 12 areas (*Fourth Report*, pp. 23-24):

> 1. It has been successfully demonstrated that team teaching can be approached as redeployment rather than as a "premium cost" program.
> 2. Achievement test results and other indications of accomplishment show that pupils learn at least as much as they do in the more traditionally organized classes.
> 3. The findings of adjustment studies of pupils participating in team teaching have been favorable.
> 4. There are many indications that most pupils, parents and teachers like team teaching.
> 5. Better use of teacher talents has been made.
> 6. Teachers have been relieved of routine clerical and housekeeping chores and have been given increased status.
> 7. Pupils have been grouped more effectively for instruction.
> 8. More efficient use of space and equipment has been made.
> 9. It has been demonstrated that clerks, aides, and technicians can play important supporting roles to teachers.
> 10. Grade lines have been successfully crossed, and, while grade barriers have not been eliminated, they are being successfully deemphasized.
> 11. Team teaching has stimulated other promising practices that are a departure from traditional organization. They include: associated or cooperative teaching, balanced roster of personnel, and the crossing of grade and room lines.
> 12. Team teaching has stimulated a wide range of other school improvement programs.

Teachers Evaluate Each Other

If teachers spent less time evaluating pupils and more time evaluating themselves, education would be improved immeasurably. In a team teaching situation, teachers tend to do just that.

---

[7] Harry A. Becker, *The Norwalk Plan of Team Teaching, Fourth Report, 1961-1962* (Norwalk, Connecticut: Board of Education, 1962), p. 3.

EXAMPLE:

When a teacher in one school was introducing the film *The Red Badge of Courage*, she gave students the plot, explained the symbolism, mentioned Henry Fleming's feelings, described his self-doubts, his struggle with conscience, and his return to battle.

In a critique of the lesson by her colleagues, this teacher was asked how she would enjoy a movie if someone in the audience leaned over and told her everything that was about to happen. It was a horrible thought. For the first time in five years of teaching, she realized that she had been killing rather than instilling a desire to learn. She recognized the entire introduction could have been used to question rather than to tell. Pupils could have been asked to look for the story line, for evidence of symbolism, for man's struggle with nature and himself. Afterwards, in small-group discussion, every idea she had previously explained could have been drawn from students anxious to express their own perceptions.

Teachers see the opportunities for professional growth as one of the greatest advantages of the team approach. Working together, they contribute to each other's development in an in-service training program that becomes a daily routine, not a special problem. Provided with an opportunity for interaction seldom matched in any other way, new and less experienced teachers develop rapidly. This has been proven in school after school— for example, in the Neeley Elementary School, Berea, Ohio, where a new teacher was hired to take the place of one team member granted emergency leave early in the school year. Under the tutelage of her teammate, the new teacher quickly became an efficient, effective teacher. Beginning teachers bring enthusiasm and new ideas straight from the college campus and in return receive guidance and practical experience from their colleagues.

Team teachers have the advantage of working together in teams to develop professional partnerships. For example, in Pittsburgh,

. . . Teaching on The Hill [the area in which schools now are using team teaching] used to be considered "Siberia." Teachers who considered themselves self-respecting shunned the assignment. Today, teacher turnover there is down 75 percent. The number of substitutes has dropped from 25 percent to 9.8 percent. Seven out of ten teaching internes say they'd like to come back after graduation (some 25 percent have already done so). No team leader has yet asked for a transfer. The only losses have been through promotion. And what of the children? Tests given early in the history of team teaching showed a skyrocketing increase in I.Q. scores in seven months. Sixth graders jumped 7.5 percentiles; fourth graders, 9.3 percentiles. "I don't believe it," says project director Hayes. "I don't trust these figures. We have the results; but they're too radical to accept at face value. Maybe the questionnaire was administered improperly. You don't get this kind of human growth in so short a time. I'll believe it if we can see the same thing two or three years from now. Check me then." [8]

Team Teaching as Preparation for College

The school system at Muskegon, Michigan, recently made a study which indicates that team teaching is more adequate than traditional instruction for meeting crucial educational needs of the future.[9]

After several years of team teaching at Muskegon High School in the fields of mathematics, science, history, and English, the school administration wondered how their graduates fared in college. Each graduate of the class of 1964 who attended college in 1965 was interviewed and asked an extensive series of questions. Because students had participated in team teaching on a voluntary basis, it was possible to compare team-taught students with products of the traditional system. More than 300 students were interviewed, divided about equally into team-taught and nonteam-taught.

When asked "What do you consider to be your strengths as a result of your high school preparation?" the following items were mentioned most frequently:

Item	Number of responses Team	Nonteam
Note taking	40	12
Budgeting of time	20	7
Adjustment to college	15	2
Good study habits	12	9
Ability to plan and organize	11	9
Listening in lectures	11	2
Knowing how to use resource materials	8	2

In response to the question "What do you consider to be your weaknesses as a result of your high school preparation?" the most frequent responses were:

---

[8] Bernard Bard, "How Team Teaching Works in Pittsburgh," *The Kiwanis Magazine*, January 1965, p. 85.

[9] Information provided through the courtesy of the Muskegon Public Schools, Muskegon, Michigan.

Item	Number of responses	
	Team	Nonteam
Poor study habits	4	24
Budgeting of time	4	15
Adjustment to college	0	10
Self-discipline	1	9
Ability to plan and organize	4	6
Note taking	0	5

On a list of items, graduates were asked to indicate those in which they had been exceptionally well-prepared by their high school. Comparative results follow:

Item	Percentage of responses	
	Team	Nonteam
Independent research	52%	26%
Note taking	85%	31%
Learning to think for yourself	53%	26%
Coping with heavy assignments	36%	10%
How to study	27%	8%
Writing term papers	34%	24%
Vocabulary	10%	18%
Taking essay tests	32%	28%
Using the library effectively	42%	25%
Organizing reading materials	29%	11%
Keeping up with outside load	25%	14%

When the graduates were asked "Do you feel you were prepared for college as a result of your high school experiences?" their responses were extremely favorable.

Item	Percentage of affirmative responses	
	Team	Nonteam
Community college	85%	82%
Colleges other than community college	95%	85%

This survey was not definitive, nor was it intended to be. However, it did answer several questions. Students prepared for college in a team process were quite happy with their preparation, were well-adjusted to college, and were more than holding their own. Muskegon, Michigan, with an excellent reputation to uphold, needed assurance they were helping and not hindering their pupils. As a result of this survey, the team program is being expanded.

61

WHY TEAM TEACH?

The three reasons given most often today for adopting team teaching are:

1. To improve staff utilization.
2. To improve use of facilities and equipment.
3. To improve instruction.

Improvements in staff utilization are readily apparent. Team teaching recognizes and encourages individual differences in teachers as well as in students. Flexibility and variation are emphasized. Repetition and duplication are shunned. Savings in time and effort are reinvested in the individual child. Extra effort is expended on planning and preparation. Talents are blended, weaknesses are minimized. Teachers assume a variety of roles and teach in their areas of interest and strength.

Common sense indicates a more economical use of public funds. When centers are established for large-group instruction and independent study, a limited amount of equipment serves a wide number of teachers and pupils. Team teachers have discovered when they move out of their self-contained rooms and share material as well as ideas, there are plenty of each to go around.

The most important "subject" in any school is the child. This makes improvement of instruction a major goal. Although team teaching does not cure poor teachers, it does give them a chance to be observed, critiqued, and improved. Working alone, many teachers have retired not with 40 years of experience, but with one year of experience repeated 40 times. Working in teams, teachers have an opportunity for 40 years of professional growth.

Team teaching is a venture in learning. It is not for the teacher or principal who feels his educational goal has been reached; it is for the person who realizes he has just begun.

A sage once remarked: "There are three kinds of educators: those who make things happen, those who watch things happen and those who wonder what happened."

We need more of the first type!

LIST OF SELECTED REFERENCES

And No Bells Ring. Team Teaching Film, Parts I and II. Washington: National Association of Secondary School Principals, NEA. Two 16 mm films show team teaching in action. 28 minutes each.

Bair, Medill and Richard G. Woodward, *Team Teaching in Action.* Boston: Houghton Mifflin Company, 1964. A report covering five years of experiences with team teaching in the Lexington, Massachusetts school system.

Beggs, David W., ed., *Team Teaching: Bold New Venture.* Indianapolis: Unified College Press, Inc., 1964. Twelve contributors define, explain, and evaluate team teaching.

————, *Instructional Materials Center: Bold New Venture.* Bloomington: Indiana University Press, 1966. Eleven chapters focus on using the instructional materials center for independent study.

Brown, Frank, *The Nongraded High School.* Englewood Cliffs, New Jersey: Prentice-Hall, Inc., 1963. A complete description of the nongraded program at Melbourne High School, Melbourne, Florida.

Bush, Robert N. and Dwight W. Allen, *A New Design for High School Education.* New York: McGraw-Hill Book Company, 1964. Includes a detailed description of flexible scheduling.

The Claremont Teaching Team Program. Claremont, California: Claremont Graduate School, 1961, 32 pp. Describes the Claremont teaching team "school within a school" concept and explains how it works in both the elementary and secondary levels of instruction.

The Cost of a Schoolhouse. New York: Educational Facilities Laboratories, Inc., 1960, 144 pp. Primarily deals with the cost of a schoolhouse and the process of planning and financing. Children, education, flexible buildings, and flexible programs are also discussed.

Davis, Harold S., compiler, *The Instructional Materials Center—An Annotated Bibliography.* Cleveland: The Educational Research Council of Greater Cleveland, 1965, 34 pp. Provides source information for administrators and librarians interested in learning more about staffing and operating an IMC.

————, *Team Teaching Bibliography.* Cleveland: The Educational Research Council of Greater Cleveland, 1964, 95 pp. A comprehensive bibliography containing an annotated books and pamphlets section. All articles are catalogued according to teaching level and subdivided by topic.

A Divisible Auditorium/Boulder City, Nevada. New York: Educational Facilities Laboratories, 1963, 23 pp. Operable walls add and subtract space quickly and automatically. The auditorium can easily be converted to a flexible combination of large-group instruction spaces.

Goodlad, John I. and Robert H. Anderson, *The Nongraded Elementary School.* New York: Harcourt Brace, 1963. A complete discourse on the rationale for and development of the nongraded elementary school. The tie-in with team teaching is discussed in some detail.

Lobb, M. Delbert, *Utilization of the Staff in Education, A Report of a Three Year Study, 1957-1960.* Jefferson County, Colorado: School District R-1, June, 1960, 30 pp. A look at the why, where, when, who, and what of team teaching in Jefferson County. This interesting report includes a section describing results.

Morse, Arthur D., *Schools of Tomorrow—Today.* Garden City, New York: Doubleday and Company, Inc., 1960. A report on educational experiments including team teaching, teachers aides, television teaching, and the ungraded primary.

National Association of Secondary-School Principals Bulletin. Vols. XLII-XLVI. January editions for 1958-1962 inclusive. Reports of staff utilization studies.

The New High School: A School for Our Times. New York City: Board of Education, 1963, 22 pp. The high school division Committee on Experimentation recommends the "need for adventuring."

Norwalk School Improvement Program, April, 1962-August, 1963. Norwalk, Connecticut: Norwalk Board of Education, 1963, 40 pp. A progress report covering 17 months of innovations in the Norwalk School Improvement Program.

Planning and Organizing for Teaching. Washington: NEA, 1963, 180 pp. Report by the NEA Project on the Instructional Program of the Public Schools. Includes several recommendations regarding team teaching.

Profiles of Significant Schools: High Schools, 1962. New York: Educational Facilities Laboratories, Inc., 1961, 86 pp. A status report on educational change and architectural consequence. Section 2 is entitled "Teaching in Teams."

Profiles of Significant Schools: Schools for Team Teaching. New York: Educational Facilities Laboratories, Inc., 1960, 63 pp. Representative examples of elementary and junior high schools designed to house team teaching programs.

Pupils, Patterns, and Possibilities: A Description of Team Teaching in Pittsburgh. Pittsburgh: Board of Education, 1961, 32 pp. The story of team teaching in Pittsburgh.

Schools for the 60's. New York: McGraw-Hill Book Company, 1964, 146 pp. This report by the NEA Project on Instruction stresses the need for research, experimentation, and innovation. Team teaching efforts are encouraged.

Time, Talent and Teachers. New York: The Ford Foundation, 1960, 49 pp. An informal presentation of several Ford Foundation staff utilization projects with an emphasis on the instructional revolution and the flexible school .

Trump, J. Lloyd and Dorsey Baynham. *Focus on Change—Guide to Better Schools.* Chicago: Rand McNally and Company, 1961. The story of several staff utilization projects, a report on the coming of a new kind of secondary education and suggestions for changes in elementary schools.

Wolfe, Arthur B., *The Nova Plan for Instruction.* Fort Lauderdale, Florida: Broward County Board of Public Instruction, 1962, 84 pp. Describes team teaching and the nongraded program at Nova High School.